Yesterday, Today, and Tomorrow

Bob Chilcott

for SSA and piano

vocal score

OXFORD
UNIVERSITY PRESS

OXFORD
UNIVERSITY PRESS

Great Clarendon Street, Oxford OX2 6DP,
United Kingdom

Oxford University Press is a department of the University of Oxford.
It furthers the University's objective of excellence in research, scholarship,
and education by publishing worldwide. Oxford is a registered trade mark of
Oxford University Press in the UK and in certain other countries

ISBN 978–0–19–356833–4

Music and text origination by Katie Johnston
Printed in Great Britain on acid-free paper by
Halstan & Co. Ltd, Amersham, Bucks.

Contents

Composer's note

In 1998 I wrote a piece for upper voices called *Look to this day!*, which included this inspiring Sanskrit text: 'Look to this day! For today well lived, makes every yesterday a dream of happiness, every tomorrow a vision of hope'. This text has stayed with me, and I suggested to the poet Georgia Way that she might use it as a starting point to write three texts for songs that express the past, the present, and the future. Georgia's poems not only translate the idea of this text in a striking and contemporary way, but also bring the energy and joy of youth to the fore. *Yesterday, Today, and Tomorrow* was written for the 2023 Crescent City Choral Festival and commissioned by the New Orleans Children's Chorus and their Director, Cheryl Dupont.

Duration: *c.*10 minutes

Commissioned by the New Orleans Children's Chorus and their Artistic Director, Cheryl Dupont, for the 2023 Crescent City Choral Festival

Yesterday, Today, and Tomorrow

1. Yesterday

Georgia Way (b. 1992)

BOB CHILCOTT

6

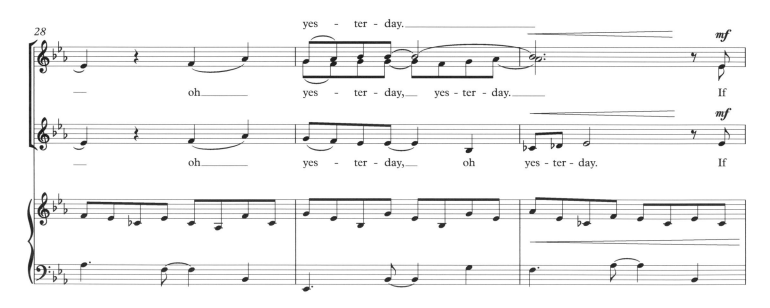

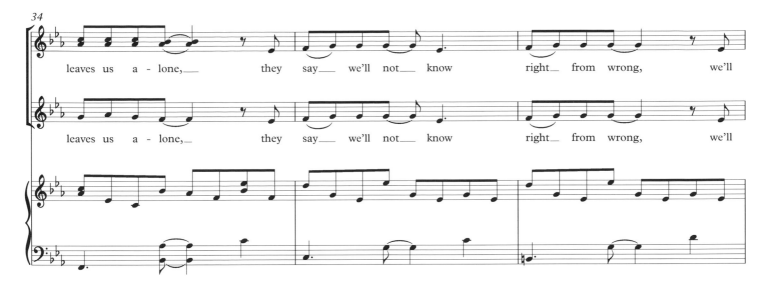

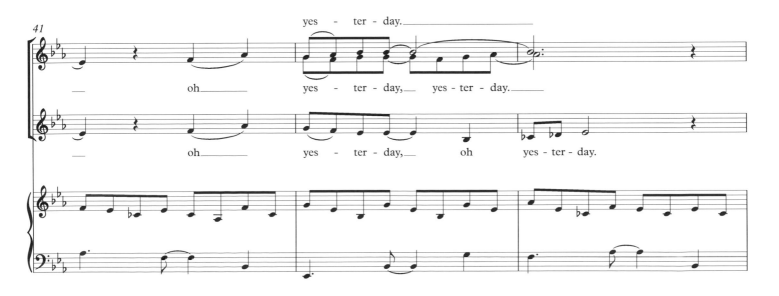

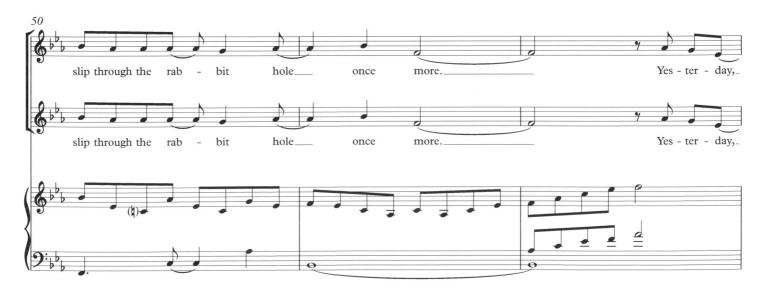

2. Today

14

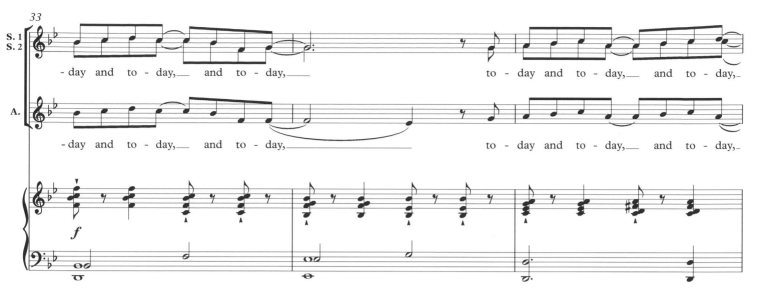

- day and to - day,___ and to - day,___   to - day and to - day,___ and to - day,___

the day,___ the day___ is light,   and youth__ is star-

- light.___

3. Tomorrow

20

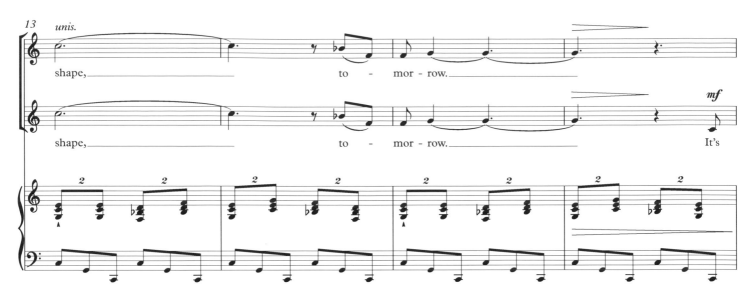

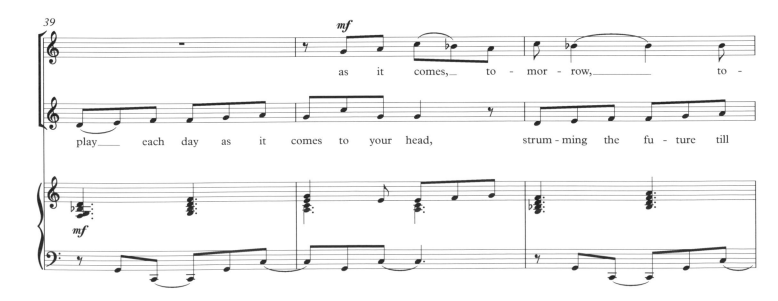

26

27

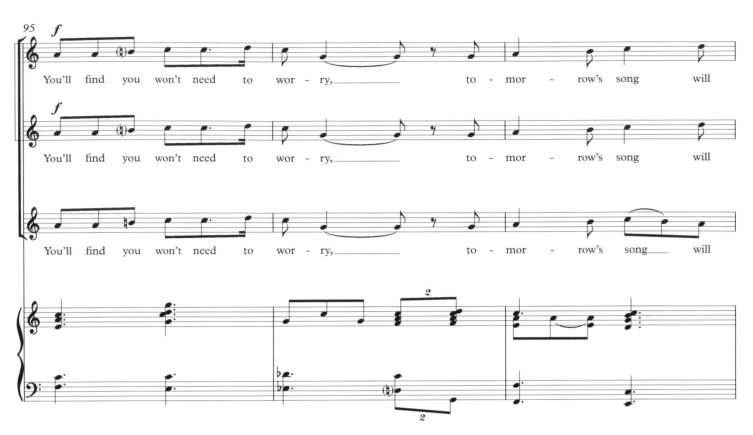

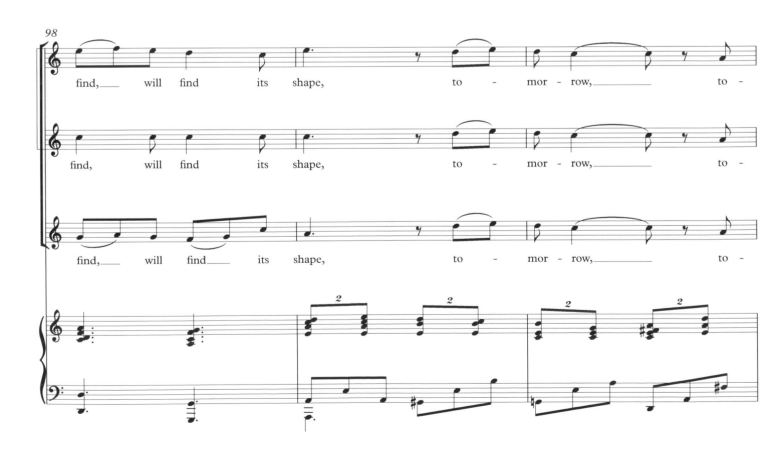